WORDSWORTH
IN A
NEW LIGHT

LONDON : HUMPHREY MILFORD
Oxford University Press

WORDSWORTH

IN A

NEW LIGHT

By EMILE ~~Hyacinthe~~ LEGOUIS

CAMBRIDGE

HARVARD UNIVERSITY PRESS

1923

100 COPIES ON HAND-MADE PAPER

TYPOGRAPHY BY BRUCE ROGERS

PRINTED AT THE HARVARD UNIVERSITY PRESS

CAMBRIDGE, MASS., U.S.A.

WORDSWORTH

IN A

NEW LIGHT

THE subject of this lecture may require some explanation, perhaps some apology. It is one of those that may be called unpleasant, since it concerns the moral transgression of a great and revered poet. Yet it by no means pretends to come as a revelation. The fact itself is now known to most readers. It has been stated and commented upon in books, reviews, and newspapers. The reading public has in recent years been informed how William Wordsworth, while he lived in France in 1792, fell in love with a French lady called Annette Vallon and had by her a daughter, to whom he gave his name, though he never would or could marry the mother.

The scandal that might attach to a story of the sort would only be aggravated by private whisperings and timid reticence. It is, on the contrary, much lessened by a thorough knowledge of the circumstances. Though the story does away with the fictitious image of a Wordsworth supernaturally free from all temptation, who found wisdom ready-made in his cradle, it confirms, on the whole, what we already know of the poet's moral soundness and human nature. From an open and plain treatment of the question his character has nothing to fear.

But before examining the tale, I beg to say how I was induced to investigate the problem.

In the last years of the last century, some time after I had published a book on the *Early Life of Wordsworth*, I called in London on a friend of mine, Thomas Hutchinson, now deceased, who was soon to make himself known as the editor of Wordsworth, Shelley, and Charles Lamb, and who had often encouraged and helped me with his advice while I was preparing the book. In the course of our talk he asked me whether I was aware of a well-established tradition in the Coleridge family that William Wordsworth, during his stay in France, had by a young French lady a *son*, who afterwards visited him at Rydal Mount. The news of that tradition, which mixed truth with some error (an error which can now be accounted for), made me regret that I had not known the fact beforehand, so as to alter some pages of my work which were flatly contradicted by it. I may even as an author expect your sympathy and compassion for some despite I felt at having been misled by former biographers. I had aimed at truth and tumbled into a pitfall. Yet, as I had then turned to other studies, I let the thing pass and allowed the story to sleep for many years, not hiding it from those who were concerned with the poet's life, but never committing it to print.

Then there came the time when Professor
George Harper of Princeton University began
to write his masterly biography of the poet.
I told him the little I knew. But no further
advance was made till he discovered among
the manuscripts in the British Museum a
series of letters written by Dorothy Wordsworth to Mrs. Clarkson, the wife of the anti-
slavery apostle, wherein clear mention was
made of a French lady named Madame Vallon, and of a daughter of hers named Caroline, whom Dorothy called her niece. The
letters also gave their Paris address.

Once furnished with this clue, Professor
Harper could give us a first sketch of the
story in his *Life of William Wordsworth*,
which came out in 1916. Having afterwards
come to France again during the war, to help
in the American Hospital at Neuilly, he de-
voted his very scanty leisure to further research, and was so fortunate as to find some
documents of great importance, such as the
birth and marriage certificates of Caroline

Wordsworth. He, moreover, identified Annette as the sister-in-law of a Madame Vallon whose memoirs of the Revolutionary times had appeared in 1913.

All these discoveries he generously imparted to me while he was in Paris; but I must confess that, though they strongly impressed me at the moment, the terrible circumstances (the war was at its darkest hour) soon drove the precise facts from my memory, leaving only the remembrance of their general interest. When Professor Harper had to leave France and return to Princeton, he regretted to leave his research only half done, and urged me to bring it to an end. But I had no such design at the time, and might never have turned to the task at all, had not the English publisher of my book on the *Early Life of Wordsworth* announced to me last year his intention of republishing that work. I answered that I owed it to the reader not to publish it again without making the corrections and additions necessitated by later discoveries.

I therefore set to the writing of an appendix on the relations between Wordsworth and Annette. For this I began to dip into our records, national and local — then into those of Paris, Orleans, and Blois. Besides the documents formerly revealed to me by Professor Harper (they were published by him last year at the Princeton University Press, under the title *Wordsworth's French Daughter*), I lighted on others which he had not the time to look for, and by degrees the French family of the Vallons assumed a definite shape before my eyes. It was, moreover, my good fortune to get into touch at last with some of the living members of that family, the descendants of Wordsworth and Annette on one side, and of Annette's brother Paul on the other.

The results of my research have lately appeared in the *Revue des Deux Mondes* of April 1 and May 1, 1922. In those articles I chiefly endeavored to make the Vallons known, as their history is eventful, full of ups

and downs, much like the career of many
heroes and heroines in Balzac's novels, whose
lives extended over the same tempestuous
times.

Here my design is not quite the same. I
chiefly mean to examine what, in the light of
these fresh documents, we are to think of
Wordsworth himself — how far they help us
to a truer idea of the man he was, and also,
it may be, of his poetry. Of the Vallons I
shall speak only so far as is necessary to make
his doings and feelings clear.

It may not be superfluous to remind you
at the start that Wordsworth was born in
1770, so that he was an old man of sixty-
seven when Queen Victoria ascended the
throne. He might have died before her accession without any important loss to his
poetry and to his glory. It was only through
his latest (and weakest) effusions, and chiefly
owing to the tendency of his biographers,
that he assumed that Victorian appearance
which is decidedly anachronistic. No bigger

mistake can be made in literary history than
the mixing up of the two epochs — the one
in which he lived and the one in which he
outlived himself and died. Wordsworth was,
to all intents and purposes, a Georgian
throughout his best years; and his youthful
conduct is to be judged according to the
standard of times separated from those of
Victoria by a gulf.

There was, as you know, great looseness of
manners in the last decades of the eighteenth
century — much corruption in the higher
spheres and much roughness among the
lower ones. This is no news to those who
have a knowledge of social history, or who
have read to some extent the biographies of
that period. There were even then, of course,
regions of great purity — nay, strictness —
in England, chiefly among the Evangelicals;
but the general tone of the country was neither refined nor even what would afterwards
have been called simply decent. Of the dif-
ference between those and later times, I will

merely give you a minute instance. You may have, I think, the whole contrast in a nutshell.

Dorothy Wordsworth, the poet's exquisite sister, writing to a friend in 1795 (she was then twenty-three), expressed herself in this way:

"A natural daughter of Mr. Tom Myers (a cousin of mine, whom I dare say you have heard me mention) is coming over to England to be educated by us."

Now, could you imagine a Victorian young lady speaking with that simplicity and ingenuous frankness of her cousin's *natural* daughter?

This is only a trifling specimen of the unconventionality of those days; but it shows the extreme naturalness of natural children under the Georges. The case was so frequent that it scarcely excited comment.

The near surroundings of Wordsworth do not appear to have been among the most strait-laced, even in these years. He will,

strangely enough, congratulate himself upon
having been

> Unchecked by innocence too delicate
> And moral notions too intolerant,
> Sympathies too contracted.

The farmers' sons, his school friends at
Hawkshead, were a rough set, as he himself
tells us. At the University of Cambridge his
fellow students were a mixed lot. The com-
plaints against the disorders and immorality
of the English universities were constant and
vehement about 1790, and the poet admits
that he was more drawn toward the good fel-
lows than the earnest plodders.

Besides, to the practical license of that period there was added, in a certain number of
minds, toward the time of the French Revo-
lution, a dogmatic enfranchisement from the
usual moral restraints. The wildest ideas
were afloat, and marriage was among the in-
stitutions assailed by several philosophers.
Young Wordsworth was impressed by more
than one subversive tenet that was to enthrall

Shelley some twenty years later. It should
not be forgotten that the two poets listened
in succession to the same master of morals—
William Godwin, the adversary of matrimony
—with similar results, though while Shelley's
transgression was known at once, that of
Wordsworth was to remain long hidden.

Picture him to yourself as he was in December, 1791, when he arrived at Orleans, a
very young man, only twenty-one years and
a half old; a B.A. of Cambridge, who had
very little money indeed, but who, in spite of
his uncles' and guardians' objections (for he
was an orphan), seemed to be in no hurry to
enter upon a regular career. He was already
a poet and a lover of nature, but he was also
a wayward youth, eager to see as much as
possible of life. No strict line of conduct
guided his steps, and no settled attachment
was there to keep him from temptation. Yet
he needed such restraints more than most,
or at least as much as any. Even his poetry
(where so little of this side of his nature has

been allowed to show itself) enables us to perceive the ardor of his blood in those years. It partly and cautiously reveals what De Quincey roughly calls Wordsworth's preternatural animal sensibility, adding that his intellectual passions, like those of all great and original poets, were founded upon it. It would be quite superfluous to give the proofs, if such a spiritualizing process had not been at work in his biography that the truth has been hidden from most readers. If we ignore the unknown Lucy, whom he was to sing in his finest verse, and for whom he felt amid the English hills "the joy of his desire," there were those daughters of Westmoreland farmers whom he visited during his Cambridge vacations, with whom the whole night sometimes passed in dances from which he came back home with fevered brain, after having felt in their company

> Slight shocks of young love-liking interspersed
> Whose transient pleasure mounted to the head
> And tingled through the veins.

And it was that very "tingling" which had
favored the birth of his poetical vocation.
In the morning after one of these dancing
nights it was that, going back home on foot
and seeing the rise of a glorious dawn, he had
had the first consciousness of his genius, and
had dedicated himself to the worship of nature. The tumult of his senses had been the
means of rousing his imaginative fire. For
the first time he had felt the truth of the deep
maxim which he uttered later:

Feeling comes in aid of feeling.

A year after, when he journeyed over the
Alps, the sublimity of the mountains had not
engrossed his enthusiasm to the point of
blinding him to the beauty of the young girls
he met on his way. The dark Italian maids
he passed along the shores of Lake Como had
stirred in him voluptuous dreams, and he was
to call up their image in that very year (1792)
in lines (suppressed by him in later editions),
the awkward and obsolete turn of which does
not prevent their warmth from being felt.

Farewell! those forms that, in thy noon-tide shade,
Rest, near their little plots of wheaten glade;
Those steadfast eyes, that beating breasts inspire
To throw the "sultry ray" of young Desire;
Those lips, whose tides of fragrance come and go,
Accordant to the cheek's unquiet glow;
Those shadowy breasts in love's soft light arrayed,
And rising, by the moon of passion swayed.

Surely the young man who wrote these lines, slightly ridiculous in form but full of fire, was not yet wholly absorbed in the contemplation of scenery. He enjoyed nature, but called out for love — love in its integrity, not the mere satisfaction of a passing fancy, for his heart was as ardent as his senses. He carried in his attachments that "violence of affection" that endeared him to his sister Dorothy. He had in his disposition all the elements that make for a great passion. He was, like the lover of Ruth, —

A youth to whom was given
So much of earth — so much of heaven,
And such impetuous blood.

Such was Wordsworth in 1792, when he met Annette Vallon, probably at Orleans,

where she may have been on a prolonged
visit to one of her brothers, Paul, a notary's
clerk in that town.

She was the sixth and last child of a sur-
geon of Blois. Her father was dead. Her
mother had married again, and she was
scarcely less abandoned to herself than the
orphan poet. She was by four or five years
William's senior, and in consequence bears
the chief responsibility in the adventure.
They may have stayed in the same boarding
house, or William may have frequented the
family with whom Annette was living.

The young Englishman did not know
much French, and yet would not go to the
expense of paying a private master. Annette is said to have been obliging, and of
her having been voluble there can be no
doubt. She helped the foreign youth with his
French. The conversation of women has al-
ways been a readier help to beginners than
that of men. Women have more leisure and
compliance. They know better how to turn

a dry task into a pleasure. Annette set the
shy young Northerner at ease by her kind-
ness — perhaps also by laughing good-
humoredly over his unpronounceable name.
She showed an interest in his affairs beyond
what the solitary youngster had for some
time been used to. He felt lonely now and
then, and thirsted for sympathy. He fell
desperately in love with her, and the mere
sight of her at her casement became the
brightest minute in each of his days.

This is no fiction — merely the plain truth,
if we admit that in his poem of *Vaudracour
and Julia* he drew on his memories of this
early love to describe the hero's first raptures.
This might be supported by strong argument;
but, for want of space, I will content myself
with quoting a few lines of the poem.

> He beheld
> A vision, and adored the thing he saw.
> Arabian fiction never filled the world
> With half the wonders that were wrought for him.
> Earth breathed in one great presence of the spring;
> Life turned the meanest of her implements,
> Before his eyes, to price above all gold;

The house she dwelt in was a sainted shrine;
Her chamber-window did surpass in glory
The portals of the dawn; all paradise
Could, by the simple passing of a door,
Let itself in upon him.

These were the first pure, innocent moments. But soon after came the fault for which the same poem furnishes us (this time in language as clumsy as the preceding verses are beautiful) with two explanations, between which we may choose the one that we think more probable. From this passage we may also infer that some obstacle stood, from the first, between them and a regular contract.

                            Whether through effect
Of some unguarded moment that dissolved
Virtuous restraint — ah! speak it, think it, not!
Deem rather that the fervent youth, who saw
So many bars between his present state
And the dear haven where he wished to be
In honourable wedlock with his Love,
Was inwardly prepared to turn aside
From law and custom, and entrust his cause
To nature for a happy end of all:
Deem that by such fond hope the youth was swayed,
And bear with their transgression, when I add
That Julia, wanting yet the name of wife,
Carried about her for a secret grief
The promise of a mother.

Substitute Annette for Julia, and you very probably have Wordsworth's own story here.

I pass over the summer months at Blois and the autumn at Orleans, all so full of passion and remorse, growing anxiety, and impending shame. The recital of events is not my object. What we wish to know is why the mutual love which surely prevailed between him and Annette did not lead to a marriage; why the poet, when a daughter was born to him on the 15th of December, gave her his name, — at least, as far as the French vicar could spell it (Wordswodsth), — but did not give it to the mother.

The simple truth seems to be this: he had neither money nor any near prospect of a career. He entirely depended on his uncles and guardians for further assistance. He had to set his case before them and get their consent to the union he meditated. He resolved to go to England for this purpose, and to come back to Annette as soon as he had

raised the necessary means. That he was
sincere in the promise he made her of a
speedy return, there can be no doubt; but, as
we shall see, public events stood in his way
and were to separate him from her for ten
years.

The scene changes. Wordsworth is back
in England. Annette is living at Blois with
her family, but, for fear of scandal, has had to
part from little Caroline, whom she has sent
to nurse some way off, but whom she visits
constantly. She carries on with Wordsworth
a copious correspondence, one specimen of
which has, curiously enough, survived. The
war which broke out between England and
France a few weeks after Wordsworth's return to his own country, caused the letter she
wrote to both William and his sister Dorothy
on March 20, 1793, to be seized by the
French police. In this letter, which never
reached him, Annette by turns implores him
to come at once and marry her according to
his promise, and supplicates him *not* to come

on account of the state of war, and because,
if he came, he might be sent to prison. To
this the fond mother adds a profuse descrip-
tion of Caroline, now three months old, but
already a prodigy of charms and intelligence
and likeness to her father. Throughout the
long letter Annette shows herself a woman of
feeling, an *âme sensible*, as only people of the
end of the eighteenth century could be. The
poor woman gushes over with love and tears,
but through the cant of the age her sincerity
remains apparent. Her passionate soul is de-
void of bitterness; her love rings as true as
her sorrow.

What did the poet do on receiving — not
this appeal, but those that had surely pre-
ceded it, and such others as could afterwards
now and then elude the police? What do we
all wish, for chivalry's sake, he might have
done? Of course, go in spite of the war, in
the teeth of danger, to Annette's relief.

The suppression in the Wordsworth family
papers of all that appertains to his French

adventure does not allow us to prove that he
did it. But it remains possible that he endeavored to do it. He must have been in
France again in the autumn of 1793, if he was
present, as he told Carlyle in 1840, at the
execution of Gorsas, the first of the Girondists to be sent to the scaffold. If we combine
this fact with an anecdote related by Alaric
Watts, which evidently mixes some reality
with much inaccuracy, Wordsworth was
then and there alarmed by a Republican
named Bailey, who told him that he would
surely be guillotined if he stayed in France
any longer; whereupon he fled back to England. The risk he had run simply by coming
at all was enormous. As soon as the Terror
had set in, it would have been sheer madness
to stay on. As a friend of the Girondists and
as an Englishman, he was doubly suspected.

Even if Wordsworth made that rash at-
tempt, as all his admirers wish it might be
proved he did, he could not, after all, go so
far as Blois, and had to leave France without

marrying (or perhaps even seeing) Annette. He could do nothing to relieve her, and he was too tender-hearted not to suffer acutely from his powerlessness. His thoughts were at that time as dark as they could be (witness his poem, *Guilt and Sorrow*, and his *Prelude*), and not for public reasons only, but also from private grief and pangs of conscience. Till 1795, at least, he is known to have wandered about England disconsolately, writing dismal verse. He ought, of course, to have accepted a situation and earned the money which he needed, not only for himself, but also to help the forsaken ones as soon as he could have access to them again. An ordinary good man would have done it, as the immediate duty. But Wordsworth was not an ordinary man: he was a poet, haunted by the demon of verse; he was, moreover, a Republican and in a state of revolt against all society. He kept waiting and fretting for many weary months, doing nothing, while the war raged on.

But, after 1795, when he had settled with his beloved sister at Racedown, his mood began slowly to alter. Poetry and nature, together with his sister's love, exerted their restoring influence. He soon felt so happy in his retreat that he could not think without some anxiety of a change that would tear him from that congenial life. His former love of France made room by degrees for the deep-set patriotism for which many poems of his are justly celebrated. He still thought tenderly of Annette and Caroline; but when that thought weighed too heavily on his heart, he found some comfort in using the famous Goethean recipe. He purged off his melancholy, his feelings of pity and remorse, by writing a number of poems on poor forsaken wives or unwedded mothers. Remember *The Ruined Cottage*, written in 1797 — the story of poor Margaret, who lived happy with her husband when the war broke out; then her husband, for lack of work, enlisted and disappeared, never to come back again. She sees her baby pine away, her garden go to waste, her cottage fall into ruins. Remember, in the *Lyrical Ballads* of 1798, *The Thorn* — the tale of Martha Ray, who was with child when Stephen Hill forsook her and married another girl. She puts her baby to death and becomes half mad with grief. She will never cease to come and moan over the heap of turf planted with a thorn where the village people believe she buried the little body.

Think chiefly of *The Mad Mother*, one of Wordsworth's most moving ballads, the song of the poor wife suckling her baby far away from the husband who deserted her — a prolonged complaint, a stirring appeal to the forgetful absent man. Had not the poet a frequent vision of another mother lulling her baby to rest, of one who could also imagine, as she did not see her lover come back, that she had been abandoned and forgotten? It is a fact that some of the themes in the song are identical with those used by Annette in her letter of March, 1793.

Thy father cares not for my breast;
'T is thine, sweet baby, there to rest;
'T is all thine own! — and, if its hue
Be changed, that was so fair to view,
'T is fair enough for thee, my dove!
My beauty, little child, is flown,
But thou wilt live with me in love;
And what if my poor cheek be brown?
'T is well for me, thou canst not see
How pale and wan it else would be.

Add to the list *Ruth* (1799), who listens to the intoxicating talk of a young adventurer from Georgia and his rapturous descriptions of the tropics. She allows him to lead her to the altar; but he soon leaves her, to resume the free wandering life he loves, and she goes mad for grief.

Thus did Wordsworth give vent to his pity, and, like most poets, he gradually freed himself from his remorse by uttering it.

On the other hand, the war went on as if it were to last forever. He was no longer the same man he had been in 1792, and from the vantage ground of distance and time he was beginning to realize that his love for Annette

had been a mistake — that they were as
separated by language, country, tastes, ideas,
and temperaments, as the poles. This dis-
covery of his altered feelings crystallized in
the beautiful Lucy poems, written soon after
the *Lyrical Ballads*, during the stay he made
in 1799 in Germany with his sister Dorothy.

She remains enigmatic after all — the
young Lucy to whose solitary cottage he used
to ride in the moonlight. We have here the
memory of a youthful love that should be
placed even before his meeting with Annette.
At that date (1799) Wordsworth is meditat-
ing his *Prelude*, and turning back to his early
years, to his native mountains, with a hope
to draw from those sources new strength and
faith. We may imagine Lucy as loved by the
Hawkshead schoolboy toward the end of his
school term, or by the Cambridge student
during one of his vacations. The importance
of the poems in this connection is that he
sends to her in her grave the assurance that
she was his truest love.

For that she had two titles, which nothing
seems now to withstand. She was a moun-
tain girl; she lived in a lovely, lonely dale.
Nature had vowed to make her a lady of her
own. Her charms would be the reflection of
the beauties of sky, clouds, springs, and woods.

> And hers shall be the breathing balm,
> And hers the silence and the calm
> Of mute insensate things.

Her other title was that she was English. It
was undoubtedly his stay in Germany, as sad
as an exile, that drew from the poet his vow
nevermore to leave his own country. The
time he had spent in France had been very
different, and he had then repined at the
necessity that drew him back to England.
But now he forswears all foreign countries.
He who lately wished France to triumph over
England now reconciles himself with his
country over Lucy's tomb.

> I travelled among unknown men
> In lands beyond the sea;
> Nor, England! did I know till then
> What love I bore to thee.

'T is past, that melancholy dream!
  Nor will I quit thy shore
A second time; for still I seem
  To love thee more and more.

Among thy mountains did I feel
  The joy of my desire;
And she I cherished turned her wheel
  Beside an English fire.

Thy mornings showed, thy nights concealed
  The bowers where Lucy played;
And thine too is the last green field
  That Lucy's eyes surveyed.

It may be that these stanzas were not aimed at Annette, but they pass her over, so to say, and, by ignoring her, pronounce her sentence. She was precisely the one who owed nothing to the soil or sky of England, the one who spoke another language, who would be an exile in an English village and wondered at by the villagers. Above all, she was town-born and town-bred; she had been used all her days to the social life of cities: she had not "the silence and the calm of mute insensate things"; she had an overflowing tongue, together with the worldly habits

which the poet now proclaims worthless if
not reprehensible; and there were in her none
of the associations that tie up a soul to nature. If ever the poet were to marry her now,
as he had once meant to do, it would be out
of duty and gratitude, but with the cer-
tainty of having spoiled his own life.

The crisis was to come in 1802, when
Wordsworth took Mary Hutchinson to wife.
Little by little his thoughts had turned back
to the sweet silent Penrith maid he had
known in his earliest years, but who had
more or less been driven from his mind by
others. The purpose of marrying her seems
to have slowly matured, and to have taken
definite shape only after his German travel.
She possesses the calm he longs for; *she* is
English and used to country life. As early as
1800, he had dedicated to her a lovely poem
and fancifully given her name to a small glade
in the woods, full of beauty and repose — an
unknown site, unvisited by travelers.

> But it is beautiful;
> And if a man should plant his cottage near,
> Should sleep beneath the shelter of its trees,
> And blend its waters with his daily meal,
> He would so love it that, in his death hour,
> Its image would survive among his thoughts;
> And therefore, my sweet Mary, this still nook,
> With all its beeches, we have named from You!

This was as good as a declaration of love at a time when the war was going on and the separation from Annette seemed destined to last forever. Seven or eight years had elapsed since he had met her, and the scanty news he may have received from her, if he received any, in the meantime showed her engaged in incessant conspiracies for the restoration of the French monarchy. The desolate unwedded mother of 1793 had soon after, under the impulse of great family misfortunes, — her brother Paul had been unjustly sentenced to death by Fouquier-Tinville, and had escaped the guillotine only by long hiding, — turned into an intrepid Chouanne, risking the jail or the scaffold by affording help to suspected royalists and per-

secuted priests. Her life had taken an inde-
pendent course, and it did not seem possible
that it should ever again combine with that
of the poet of nature.

Thus had Wordsworth been led away from
Annette to a sort of precontract with Mary
Hutchinson, when, toward the end of 1801,
peace began to be talked of. The prelim-
inaries of the Peace of Amiens allowed the
intercourse between the two countries to be
resumed; and after years of interruption, letters from France began to reach the Wordsworths again. Then came the dilemma. We
read in Dorothy's journal of March 21, 1802:
"A rainy day. William very poorly. Two
letters from Sara [Mary Hutchinson's sister],
and one from Annette. . . . We resolved to
see Annette, and that William should go to
Mary."

Wordsworth behaved bravely and openly
in these difficult circumstances. He told
Mary — perhaps he had done so already —
all about the past, and, though determined

to marry her, he would first see Annette and
her child. There was no longer any hesita-
tion about his future conduct. The proof is
given by his *Farewell* to his Grasmere or-
chard, in which he promises it to bring back
with him the sweet young maid, now his betrothed. But he went first with Dorothy to
Gallow Hill near Scarborough, on a visit to
Mary; then, with Dorothy again, he turned
to Calais, where Annette and Caroline had
appointed to meet them. They were to spend
four weeks together in that town.

A singular thing, that month of August
passed with Annette at Calais while Mary
was awaiting her betrothed in Yorkshire.
The conversations they had together are not
known to us. What we know for certain is
that there was no renewal of the former loves,
and yet no break in their affection. Every-
thing seems to have passed simply, gently,
quietly, without either transports or out-
breaks. We catch the tone of those inter-
views from a note in Dorothy's diary: "We

found Annette and Caroline chez Madame
Avril dans la rue de la Tête d'Or. . . . We
walked by the seashore almost every evening with Annette and Caroline, or William
and I alone." And she goes on to describe a
beautiful night upon the pier, with Caroline,
"who was delighted." It was on that oc-
casion that Wordsworth wrote one of his
most famous sonnets — the only one of his
poems that relates to his French daughter:

It is a beauteous Evening, calm and free;
The holy time is quiet as a Nun
Breathless with adoration; the broad sun
Is sinking down in its tranquillity;
The gentleness of heaven is on the sea:
Listen! the mighty being is awake,
And doth with his eternal motion make
A sound like thunder — everlastingly.
Dear Child! dear Girl! that walkest with me here,
If thou appear'st untouched by solemn thought,
Thy nature is not therefore less divine:
Thou liest in Abraham's bosom all the year;
And worshipp'st at the Temple's inner shrine,
God being with thee when we know it not.

Surely there is nothing in this pious ef-
fusion, so full of biblical and religious evo-

cations, to betray the presence of a natural daughter of the poet. That is why many critics thought Wordsworth had apostrophized his own sister — regardless of Dorothy's known exquisite sensibility to natural aspects. To us, who are better informed, that almost sacerdotal blessing offers a striking example of the way in which Wordsworth was apt to solemnize the most profane passages of his life. It may either irritate or amuse readers averse from all uncalled-for and inopportune solemnity. There is indeed a wonderful forgetfulness of contingencies, a rare lack of self-compunction in the father, a fragile sinner, who transforms himself into a sovereign pontiff.

But the words in the sonnet which are of greatest import to us are "untouched by solemn thought," which furnish us with a key to the imaginative disagreement between the Wordsworths and not only Caroline, but also, and still more, Annette. To be sure, Caroline was a ten-year-old romp, who was

readier to skip and play on Calais pier than
to contemplate with august emotions the
setting of the sun in the sea. All we know of
her tends to prove that she was playful and
lively, more sociable than contemplative.
Annette, like her daughter, was ill-made for
prolonged ecstasies before aspects of nature.
Her mind soon turned back to her ordinary
cares, to her friends at Blois, to the political
intrigues she had left in suspense to revisit
her former lover. Wordsworth and she now
had only one common feeling, their hatred
of Bonaparte; and even in this they differed,
since they hated him for diametrically op-
posite reasons: Wordsworth execrated him
as the man who was doing away with the
Republic, Annette as the extinguisher of
royalist hopes, the Consul who, instead of
restoring the Bourbons, was preparing the
accession of a new dynasty.

We may imagine their conversations, or
rather Annette's long soliloquies wherein she
poured out the tales of her conspiracies as

an adept of the Chouannerie. Wordsworth
might well admire her bravery and self-sacri-
fice, but he felt that her pursuits and aims
were almost infinitely distant from his own.
Of his poetry she could understand nothing.
There was the barrier of language between
them.

Add to this the change made by time in the
two lovers. Annette was now over thirty-six
and William only thirty-two. He might still
call himself young — which she no longer
was. Besides, the main current of her love
had long turned away from her lover to her
daughter. Her part in life had been determined in the course of their long separation.
She was to go on bringing up Caroline, more
truly hers than William's. Caroline should
stay with her, remain French, speak the language of her native land.

These are some of the probable reasons
which decided them to resume their inde-
pendence and free each other from the vows
and promises they had exchanged in 1792.

The momentous year 1802 was the crisis of
their love, the parting of the ways — though
not in anger, for they were to remain true
friends to the end. True friends, but never
husband and wife. Annette would go back
to Blois with her daughter, as Madame William or Widow William. Wordsworth might
marry Mary Hutchinson. His former love
would not stand in the way of the quiet union
he now had in view.

The rest of the story need not be told here.
It is of less importance as regards Wordsworth's feelings. Enough has been said to
allow you to appreciate his conduct. His
responsibilities are singularly diminished by
the pressure of circumstances. It was the
suddenness of the war rather than his own
will that prevented him from making immediate amends for his youthful error. It was
the long duration of the war that made him
turn his thoughts toward another woman,
when the ten years elapsed since 1792 had
almost changed his identity. He did not hide

the past from the wife he elected after a long delay; and, on the other hand, he knew how to turn his former beloved into a friend for life.

Whatever sentence is passed by you upon his transgression, is it not true that a knowledge of the circumstances is likely to mitigate your verdict?

One word of private confession as a conclusion.

All the time I have been delving into that story, I have felt some doubt and uneasiness about the good of such an investigation.

Was not I wrong in rescuing from oblivion what had been purposely hidden? Was there not a kind of indiscretion in revealing the youthful irregularity of a poet I admired and revered? He and his first biographer had taken great pains to do away with all that in his life which might not be edifying. The educative tendency is in him manifest, perhaps beyond what we find in any other great poet. To dwell on the sage's transgression was not only to act against his desire, but to undermine his beneficent authority. Why should historians be urged on by that spirit of inquiry which ruins all inspiring and edifying legends? After all, Wordsworth is chiefly a name for a certain number of poems destined to raise or comfort the souls of men. Why should we stir doubts as to the absolute perfection of the nature-sent messenger, instead of simply absorbing or interpreting his message? Might not edification be the aim of criticism as well as of poetry? Ought not truth to be made subservient to a higher object? Is truth so absolute a good by itself?

Yet the critic, though he may now and then be made uneasy by these considerations, cannot long be checked by them. No thought of immediate utility can keep him from his wonted course. He cannot remain quiet and silent when he knows he has accepted or propagated an erroneous statement. It is even impossible for him to put up with such omissions as deform the image of truth.

He is, moreover, conscious that at some time or other murder will out; and he believes that the greatest drawback to a character is not a frankly told error of conduct, but the late and sudden revelation of it after years of silence. And even then, when it is discovered, it will be the less damaging to the reputation of a man of sound nature and sterling worth, if investigated with thoroughness and stated without fear.